Effective Debriefing – The Key to Learning

Teresa Williams

BACIE
British Association for Commercial and Industrial Education
16 Park Crescent, London W1N 4AP

© Teresa Williams 1991

The materials that appear in this book may be reproduced for educational/training activities. There is no requirement to obtain special permission for such uses. We do, however, ask that the following statement appears on all reproductions:

'Reproduced from *Effective Debriefing – the Key to Learning* by Teresa Williams, published by BACIE, 1991.'

This permission statement is limited to purchasers reproducing the materials for educational or training events. Systematic or large-scale reproduction or distribution – or inclusion of items in publications for sale – may be carried out only with prior written permission from the publisher.

British Library Cataloguing in Publication Data
Williams, Teresa
    Effective debriefing.
    1. Industrial training
    I. Title II. British Association for Commercial &
Industrial Education
658.312404

ISBN 0-85171-096-4

Printed by Gwynne Printers, Hurstpierpoint, Sussex

My sincere thanks to Ben Rawlings for helping me with the drafts of this manual.

Thanks also to my husband, Steve, who has listened patiently and helped me to develop my ideas on debriefing.

Preface

Over the years I have found that many new or inexperienced trainers have asked me 'what do you do after you have run a learning activity?'. The variety and imagination which can be brought to this aspect of helping people to learn is often lacking.

My aim in compiling this manual is to share with both experienced and inexperienced trainers some of the styles and approaches which I have used and found to be effective. For those who are very new to debriefing learning activities I hope it will dispel some of the mystique which often surrounds the subject.

Contents

	Page
Introduction	7

Part One: General notes for the debriefer

What does effective debriefing depend on?	11
What can be achieved by debriefing?	12
Trainer styles in debriefing	14
Size of group for debriefing	15
Discussion groups in general	17

Part Two: Giving and receiving feedback

General guidelines to consider when giving feedback	21
General guidelines to explain to participants on how to receive feedback	23
Participants' reactions to feedback	24

Part Three: Activities for debriefing

Style 1 Charting morale	29
Style 2 Sketching feedback	32
Style 3 Meeting review	35
Style 4 Involved / frustrated	37
Style 5 Debriefing planning	39
Style 6 Good and bad points	41
Style 7 Task and process	43
Style 8 Situation analysis	45
Style 9 Question and answers	47
Style 10 With a leader and an observer	49

Part Four: Questions to ask

Topic questions

Examples of questions you can use when debriefing the planning of an activity or task	53
Examples of questions you can use when debriefing the problem solving aspects of an activity or task	55
Examples of questions you can use when debriefing the teamwork during an activity or task	58
Examples of questions you can use when debriefing the leadership of an activity or task	60
Examples of questions you can use when debriefing the monitoring and control of an activity or task	62
Examples of questions you can use when debriefing the decision making which took place during an activity or task	64

General questions

Examples of general questions you can use during debriefing	66

Welcome to .... + Impact programme ....

* Staff - (tutors)
         (support)

* Working here - indoors + outside
              - Cragwood House
              - out + about countryside

All with <u>aim</u> of <u>learning about</u> ⎧ yourself
                                         ⎨ how you manage
                                         ⎩ how others manage

(Diagram - learning environment)

* So what happens - Projects - Opportunities
                    Review - commitment
                           - participate
                           - prepared to talk, give/receive
                           - perceptions
                           - week goes <u>very</u> quick

* Finish by leaving here having learnt enough to manage yourself and other people more effectively, structure on Friday morning to try + support you

* Hotel - sort problems out immediately
        - Rooms, wet gear
        - Fire - assemble car park
_____

So what do we talk about ...... Task   nuts + bolts
                                     = specifics of job
                                ↓   - what are you here to improve
                                Management method - problem solving skills
                                ↓   eg defining problem / making decisions
                                                      listening, delegating
                                Interpersonal skills - what you actually do + say + how this affects
others perceptions - how do you feel about task/team/performance (behaviours/feelings/emotions)

Introduction

This manual will help any trainer or teacher who uses activities or exercises during their training sessions. It is particularly aimed at those involved with Management Development although the ideas and techniques will be relevant to a wide range of applications. It gives a variety of methods for reviewing what was learnt. It does not specifically cover end of day or end of course reviews although many of the methods could be easily adapted for those purposes.

You may find it helps participants to review activities using different methods at different times for the following reasons.

1. Some participants find it difficult to learn from or appraise an activity and need a fairly structured approach.
2. Over a long course or training event participants appreciate variety and imagination to stimulate thought.
3. There is a need to trigger different learners in different ways because of the different ways in which we all prefer to learn. There is the need to stimulate learners who may prefer the abstract, the concrete, the use of diagrams, the written or spoken word, or the need for quiet reflection.
4. There is a need to operate with varying levels of trust and confidence among participants.
5. Different learning objectives may make some approaches more successful than others.
6. The desire to appeal to participants' long term memory may influence the choice of methods.
7. Culture, status, experience and commitment to the learning process all affect the acceptability and effectiveness of any particular method of review.

Aim of the manual

The aim of this manual is to identify the wide variety of methods which can be used when conducting learning reviews. Debriefing can be one of those rather mystical subjects; although it is commonly seen as being one of the most important parts of a learning activity, there is little help available for the inexperienced debriefer except from a professional training course. Many debriefers are only aware of the one or two methods which their colleagues use. This means their methods lack variety and lose impact.

Reading this manual will not be a substitute for practice and experience, but I hope it will help you to plan how you are going to conduct a debriefing session with greater clarity and confidence. For those who do not have the support of an experienced colleague it will give you some ideas.

© Teresa Williams 1991, from 'Effective Debriefing – The key to learning', published by the British Association for Commercial and Industrial Education, 1991.

For the inexperienced debriefer the manual offers a step by step approach which can be followed until you have the confidence and experience to design your own methods. For the experienced debriefer this manual offers the chance to develop new approaches.

The manual is divided into four parts. The first provides some general notes and guidance for the debriefer. The second part deals specifically with giving and receiving feedback.

The third part offers examples of different debriefing activities. In each example you will find the following guidance:
- A general description of the method
- A description of possible applications
- Suggestions on how long to allow
- A list of important considerations
- A step by step example of using it
- A list of variations

The fourth part provides examples of questions for use in different circumstances.

Please feel free to read through, modify and adapt the ideas to meet the particular learning needs of your participants.

You may photocopy parts of this manual for teaching/training purposes only.

© Teresa Williams 1991, from 'Effective Debriefing – The key to learning', published by the British Association for Commercial and Industrial Education, 1991.

Part One

General notes for the debriefer

© Teresa Williams 1991, from 'Effective Debriefing – The key to learning', published by the British Association for Commercial and Industrial Education, 1991.

What does effective debriefing depend on?

Participants are often so involved in an experience that they need guidance on how to learn from what has taken place. They need help to step back and reflect upon what has happened and what can be learned.

Debriefing provides the opportunity to help this take place. Many individuals, regardless of intelligence, are unable to get the most from an experience unless thay have help from a competent debriefer. A few simple activities and learning experiences have very obvious learning points and do not need laborious debriefing. Most activities however are quite complex and need to be analysed. This analysis may be conducted in a variety of ways depending on the depth of the analysis and the preferences of the participants.

The list below summarises some of the factors on which an effective debriefing depends.

1. A considerable amount of time is needed. Often the debriefing takes as much or more time as the activity itself.
2. A debriefer needs to identify when to direct, when to lead, and when to stand back and let the group conduct the review.
3. Planning the review session is vital. So often the introduction, the main activity and the overall conclusion are planned but the debriefing is neglected or left to chance.
4. It is essential to give a clear explanation of the purpose of an activity before it takes place.
5. Each part of the course needs clear learning objectives. These may be set by the participants, their managers, or the tutor but must be explained before training commences.
6. A clear explanation should be included of how debriefing relates to the other parts of the course, including how long the debriefing will take, and what might be achieved by the end of it.
7. Observers need to be well briefed not only on what and how to observe but on how to feed back their observations. They will need to be guided on how to give their feedback. Clear ground rules on how to give and receive feedback are essential.
8. An atmosphere of trust and a setting where participants feel they can give and receive useful feedback are essential. These may take time and encouragement. They cannot be rushed.
9. The debriefer must be prepared to deal with the unexpected. Considerable flexibility is required. It can be very damaging to leave a thought process or question unresolved merely because it is time to move on to the next stage of the course. You may destroy your credibility or at best be seen to be avoiding a difficult question.

© Teresa Williams 1991, from 'Effective Debriefing – The key to learning', published by the British Association for Commercial and Industrial Education, 1991.

What can be achieved by debriefing

There are a wide variety of objectives which can be met by effective debriefing. These include focusing on the process of how participants worked on the task, the task itself, analysing assumptions, and looking at the effects of an individual's behaviour on others. More details on these possible objectives are given below.

1. Effective debriefing can establish exactly what happened in a chronological order. Many participants become so involved with their part that they are not aware of the total sequence of events. Different participants may see what happened in entirely different ways depending on their briefs, pre-conceived ideas, personal input etc.
2. Debriefing provides an ideal opportunity for discussing factual/technical information about the subject in question. This may be factual information about the technicalities of the task or about the methods and skills involved.
3. It helps participants to de-role. This means helping them to move away from the role or character they played in the activity and to move back to reality. This helps participants to resume their normal style and behaviour if this changed as a result of taking part in an activity.
4. Where there is a correct or most logical way to do things then deviations need to be pointed out and corrected where necessary. Equally important is the identification of what has been done correctly and the giving of praise. This feedback may be especially important where specific procedures or methods must be employed for reasons of safety, consistency, best practice or to meet legal requirements.
5. It can provide a safe forum for airing feelings generated during a learning activity eg extreme highs and lows, anger, frustration or satisfaction. In many cases further learning cannot take place until these feelings have been expressed and dealt with in a constructive way.
6. Part of the debriefing process may be identifying and analysing the assumptions, rationale, pre-conceived ideas or bias which participants brought to a learning activity. Making participants aware of these can be essential if participants are to be able to explore usefully and constructively other ideas or approaches to the topic they have been working on.
7. After some learning activities it may be important to focus on the process(es) which took place during the activity. Participants often need considerable help in looking at *how* things happened rather than *what*

© Teresa Williams 1991, from 'Effective Debriefing – The key to learning', published by the British Association for Commercial and Industrial Education, 1991.

actually happened. Where the objectives are to develop skills or modify attitudes then the time spent at the debriefing stage looking at the process rather than the factual or technical side gives great benefits.

8. An important skill which participants can develop at the debriefing stage is feeding back observations in a constructive and acceptable way. These reviewing and feedback skills can then be used back at work regardless of whether participants are involved in technical or managerial positions.

9. Debriefing is sometimes used to evaluate the success or failure of the results of an activity. Participants may need help in working on how they are going to define and judge success or failure, what criteria they regard as most useful (and why), and comparing results to original objectives.

10. When developing managerial skills, debriefing gives participants the opportunity to give and receive information about the effect their behaviour has on others. This helps individuals to draw their own conclusions about the appropriateness and effectiveness of different types of behaviour in particular situations. Doing this helps participants to become more aware of their impact on others.

11. The tutor is able to raise specific points if they are not naturally drawn out by participants.

12. At debriefing time both trainers and participants have the opportunity to consider the transfer and application of learning points to real situations back at work. Some participants need special help at this stage in recognising the ways in which certain facts, ideas, approaches or skills may be relevant to their area of work.

13. During the debriefing, points may be identified which relate to ideas learnt during previous activities. The tutor should be able to help participants to draw everything together to form a total picture or concept.

14. Debriefing can be used to help participants relate the points learnt to their individual learning objectives.

15. After some learning activities there may be a need to help participants to assess alternative strategies, approaches, decisions or ideas before coming to any conclusions.

16. Many participants find it useful to assess the advantages, disadvantages, potential risks or benefits of a chosen course of action at the debriefing stage before coming to any conclusions.

17. Exploring the effects of emotions on both the group and individuals is a very fruitful area for some participants. So often these important factors are neglected in discussions. Behaviour resulting from strong emotions can have a very potent effect on the results of an activity.

18. A good debriefing session helps participants to establish a firm foundation for future development, experimentation and decision making.

© Teresa Williams 1991, from 'Effective Debriefing – The key to learning', published by the British Association for Commercial and Industrial Education, 1991.

Trainer styles in debriefing

There is no single correct debriefing style. Flexibility and adaptability to the needs of the participants are key requirements. Those involved with debriefing need to be aware of the effect different styles have on participants. Listed below are three styles and their advantages and problems.

Tight control and unstructured

A very common form of debriefing is where the debriefer controls the session but in an unstructured way. This lack of structure is usually a result of little thought having been given to this aspect of the course. The debriefer does whatever seems to be a good idea at the time – often a short discussion. The success of this usually depends on participants being able and prepared to volunteer useful points without guidance. A trainer using this style with less responsible or less interested groups will often find that they appear to be unresponsive and superficial.

Tight control and structured

Another form of debriefing is a highly directive, tightly structured and tightly controlled session. It centres around some general questions on which participants are asked to focus their attention. This usually takes the form of a pre-arranged list of items which the debriefer wants to make certain are covered. It is useful when time is short, when there is a list of right or wrong points or procedures to be identified, or where the group is less able to contribute to the learning process of their own accord.

Participant-centred and gently guided

It is becoming increasingly recognised that non-directive, participant-centred modes of debriefing can be very effective in certain situations. This is especially true in the area of management skills development. In this mode the debriefer, having set the ground rules for constructive feedback, acts more as a facilitator, guiding and steering the session, helping participants to keep to relevant issues, and posing questions to explore issues which would otherwise get missed.

This requires debriefers to have highly developed skills in group dynamics, communications, counselling, conflict handling and observation rather than the standard presentation or instructional skills.

© Teresa Williams 1991, from 'Effective Debriefing – The key to learning', published by the British Association for Commercial and Industrial Education, 1991.

Size of group for debriefing

Participants on their own

There is much scope for individual participants to benefit from some time on their own completing their own self assessment and private review. For some types of learners this is just as necessary and as effective as traditional group debriefing sessions.

The tutor who normally takes the traditional debriefing role still has an important part to play in helping participants to get the most from their review time. The debriefer can help by guiding individuals on what to consider, for how long, and what to consider doing with the information at the end of that time.

For example, the individual could consider any or all of the following:
- the effectiveness of their own contribution
- the effect other people's behaviour had on them
- reasons for success or failure
- analysis of their criteria for judging success

Individuals can be encouraged to clear their thoughts and ideas by:
- making checklists
- deciding who they would like to talk to and how they would like that person to help them
- deciding how the rest of the group could help them during future activities
- deciding how they are going to ask others for help
- preparing to make a learning contract with someone else

In pairs

Even if participants have been involved in some sort of activity in a larger group, the debriefing can take place in pairs. This may be one observer to one active participant or two active participants debriefing each other. The pairs can be self selected or specially paired. Matching pairs specially can be useful where you want participants to benefit from having someone who can meet their needs. For example, a shy person may need someone who can draw them out. The person who draws them out may benefit by having a good listener which the shy person may be.

Debriefing in pairs can be useful for participants who feel the need for other people's comments and ideas but lack the confidence or confidentiality to work in larger groups. Shy or timid individuals may feel easier about expressing their

© Teresa Williams 1991, from 'Effective Debriefing – The key to learning', published by the British Association for Commercial and Industrial Education, 1991.

concerns. It is ideal for comparing perceptions about what took place, getting feedback on those perceptions, as well as giving and receiving support and encouragement.

Small groups

Many training activities take place in small groups of up to 8 participants. The debriefing can take place by keeping this group intact and having a tutor or participant taking a co-ordinating role. It is particularly appropriate where you want to debrief a whole team together to look at team behaviour.

The debriefing can take place with or without the help of observers. It can be helpful to get each team member's point of view of a critical happening during an activity. There is ample opportunity to let them find out how the same happening affected different people in different ways.

Large groups

Groups of over 8 substantially reduce the chance for individual participation in a group debriefing session. It often alienates shy or quiet individuals. The session usually needs to be more structured and more tightly controlled by a debriefer.

This type of debriefing session is likely to be used for general or superficial debriefings or where the subject matter is highly factual. It is less likely to be successful for debriefing skills and feelings. There is unlikely to be enough trust, commitment, sensitivity or security for participants to give and receive more personal types of feedback effectively.

© Teresa Williams 1991, from 'Effective Debriefing – The key to learning', published by the British Association for Commercial and Industrial Education, 1991.

Discussion groups in general

The most common method of debriefing a learning activity is to hold a discussion which is led and controlled by a tutor. This can be very useful so long as the tutor provides the right structure and the right amount of control for the group of participants.

Sometimes it is quite appropriate for participants to lead the discussion with the tutor taking a background role. Occasionally you may even decide that participants should debrief themselves without a tutor present.

The notes below give some guidance on what type of discussion group is appropriate. You can then look at Parts Three and Four to choose a specific method or set of questions as the basis of the discussion.

Before choosing a discussion group

Consider whether participants are used to holding productive discussions. How much help and guidance will they need?

Will they be willing to exchange ideas and examples?

Will they be prepared to listen to each other's ideas?

How much time do you have?

How much control and structure do they need?

Discussions can be tightly structured and tightly controlled or loosely structured and loosely controlled.

Your skills

You will need to be a good listener, able to pick up the salient points being put forward and to ask clarifying questions where necessary.

You do not need to speak a lot. If the group is able to keep to the point and is giving everyone a chance to speak, let them continue to learn from each other.

You will need to help them to recognise important issues or valuable learning points. Help them to summarise at intervals.

You should draw out quiet or shy participants if appropriate, and, if there is a problem with dominant participants help the group to handle the situation.

Using a discussion group

If you decide to use a discussion group you will need to do the following.
1. Indicate clearly what a discussion group is and what you expect from the participants. Explain how they can learn from each other.

© Teresa Williams 1991, from 'Effective Debriefing – The key to learning', published by the British Association for Commercial and Industrial Education, 1991.

2. Explain your role and how you will help.
3. Give or agree the objectives of the discussion. Explain clearly what you want them to discuss and what sort of results you expect.

    eg 'Discuss the implications of . . .   . . . for you back at work.'
    eg 'Discuss the effects of . . . which you found helped or hindered you during the activity.'

    This will give more direction than asking them to 'discuss planning' which does not say whether you mean the advantages or difficulties.
4. Give or agree a deadline for completing the discussion.
5. Open the discussion or encourage a participant to lead.
6. Make sure important points being raised are noted where appropriate.

Things that can hinder a discussion group

- Participants who are afraid they will receive criticism or ridicule.
- Those who are not interested in the subject and are not prepared to join in to help others.
- Those who feel they have the right answers and are not prepared to listen to alternative points of view.
- Participants who have physical impediments of speech may feel embarrassed.
- Discussion groups can be difficult for the deaf or hard of hearing unless special provisions are made.
- Some learners need time to reflect and consider new ideas. They may find it difficult to respond quickly or to 'think on their feet'.
- Lack of time can prevent learning taking place. If a discussion group is stopped before participants have explored the subject in a reasonable amount of depth then the outcome is usually superficial.

© Teresa Williams 1991, from 'Effective Debriefing – The key to learning', published by the British Association for Commercial and Industrial Education, 1991.

Part Two

Giving and receiving feedback

Before using a learning activity you should spend some time with participants on the subject of giving and receiving feedback. This will help the process to be of maximum value rather than being seen by the participants as a threatening and useless experience. Adapt and use the points given in this section to discuss with participants how they are going to give and receive feedback.

© Teresa Williams 1991, from 'Effective Debriefing – The key to learning', published by the British Association for Commercial and Industrial Education, 1991.

General guidelines to consider when giving feedback

Feedback and subsequent learning is likely to remain at a very superficial level unless the debriefer ensures that participants feel safe to admit to, and talk about, mistakes and weaknesses. They must feel that they can trust the other people present to respect the confidences which are being discussed. All participants including the debriefer need to operate in an open and honest way.

In order to create this sort of constructive atmosphere, the rules and guidelines need to be clearly set out by the debriefer. These should include:

1. Receptiveness of the receiver

The debriefer in charge of the overall debriefing process must guide participants who have been involved in a group activity in choosing an appropriate time to give feedback to each other or to the leader. The debriefer must encourage participants to consider what type and depth of feedback the receiver will be able and willing to accept or cope with. Feedback needs to be given in a way that the receiver can understand and identify with. Specific examples rather than generalisations usually help. Using the receiver's name and speaking directly to him/her is important to help the receiver recognise that the feedback is directly relevant to him/her.

2. Quality of the feedback

Offer observations which are descriptive, factual and accurate. Judgements and evaluations are best made by the receiver not the giver. Focus on the behaviour shown and its observed side effects rather than personal qualities. Feedback is also generally more helpful when it focuses on individual strengths rather than weaknesses (unless specifically asked for in relation to a personal learning goal). Concentrate on things that the receiver is likely to be able to influence or change.

3. Attitude of the giver

A caring and sincere approach is a necessity. The giver must limit the feedback to what the receiver could usefully hear about rather than take the opportunity to talk about everything noted down. It is also important that the giver does not

---

© Teresa Williams 1991, from 'Effective Debriefing – The key to learning', published by the British Association for Commercial and Industrial Education, 1991.

simply 'get everything off his or her chest' or talk about a 'hobby horse' without considering its effect on the receiver.

The giver should take care not to stick too long on any point but should recognise when a point has been understood and move on to the next point. Where feedback is given in a group situation participants should take care not to cut others off from making contributions by dominating the conversation. It is also an easy mistake for givers to become defensive when the receiver asks for clarification or examples to back up what has been said.

© Teresa Williams 1991, from 'Effective Debriefing – The key to learning', published by the British Association for Commercial and Industrial Education, 1991.

General guidelines to explain to participants how to receive feedback

1. Try to think about the information which is being offered in a constructive way. Consider it as free information which you can choose to ignore or accept. Whether you accept the feedback as a point of view or as a factual observation it is still up to you to decide whether or how you are going to use it.
2. Remember that someone else's perceptions about the effect of certain behaviour or idea is not necessarily right or wrong. It is worth noting however, what their perception is, why it is so, and what implications it may have.
3. Take time to form your conclusions from the feedback you receive. Do not be rushed into announcing radical changes in ideas or behaviour. If you are to succeed in making changes you must feel committed and be prepared to change habits which may have been established over many years.
4. Arguing or disagreeing with anyone will not add to the information you receive. It may instead alienate the giver and make them less likely to give you feedback in the future. You should decide later whether to accept or reject the information. While it is being given just try to absorb what is being said.
5. Ask for examples or clarification if you are not certain about what is being said. Ask for factual information if generalisations are being offered.
6. Recognise that you may not like what is being said. Some points may make you feel uncomfortable or upset. It is not easy to accept that what you think is right or the correct approach may not be perceived as such by others. Try to separate your emotional reaction to the information from the genuineness and relevance of the comment.

© Teresa Williams 1991, from 'Effective Debriefing – The key to learning', published by the British Association for Commercial and Industrial Education, 1991.

Participants reactions to feedback

The debriefer has to be aware that participants may have a variety of reactions to feedback. Such reactions can include:

Total acceptance of new ideas with a positive attitude.

Rejection of ideas or mental withdrawal	• because they think they are irrelevant • because they just don't want to know • for self protection • because it's too much like hard work to change • because they are afraid of losing face by admitting mistakes
Feeling emotionally hurt	• taking things very personally
Surprise	• because they never thought of something from that viewpoint before • it may be a total shock that a point applies to them personally
Satisfaction, reassurance	• their approach is on the right lines
Looking for support	• for the way ahead • for some hand holding and sympathy
Scepticism	• healthy or otherwise
Confusion	• previous milestones or anchor points may now be in question • previous facts may be found to be wrong or not very useful • other participants describe similar experiences which had different outcomes
A need for detail	• more examples needed • clarification in detail

© Teresa Williams 1991, from 'Effective Debriefing – The key to learning', published by the British Association for Commercial and Industrial Education, 1991.

Overreaction
- from trying to absorb and deal with many new points all at once
- exaggerated responses or attempts to do things differently where only slight modification is appropriate

An inability to take points from the learning activity and to relate them back to work.

© Teresa Williams 1991, from 'Effective Debriefing – The key to learning', published by the British Association for Commercial and Industrial Education, 1991.

Part Three

Activities for debriefing

The following activities show a range of approaches which you can adapt for your own use. Each one provides:
- a general description
- applications
- guidance on time
- suggested number of participants
- any other considerations to take into account
- step by step method
- variations

The copyright allows photocopying for teaching/training purposes.

Style 1: Charting morale

General description

This method of debriefing is useful at any stage during a course when you want to find out about individual participant's morale.

Applications

This method can be used immediately after an exercise, at the end of a day, or at any point where you want to get more information on how participants are feeling. It can be used to feed back the level of their morale to tutors and/or other participants. Sometimes it is useful to have it as the preliminary part of the debriefing process in order to help the debriefer decide on the most appropriate next step.

Time

If used at a fairly superficial level then the charting process can be completed in about 20 minutes. However, you may need to allow considerably longer than this if participants want and need to talk about how they are feeling, and why, in more detail.

Number of participants

Up to 10 participants.

Other considerations

When deciding to use this method consider whether enough trust has developed between participants for any feedback to be honest. Participants need to feel safe and secure for this method to work.

This method of debriefing often results in participants wanting to talk about factors which led to their current level of morale. This can be very important and a lot can be learned by participants doing so. Therefore it is important that you only use this method when there is the flexibility in the programme to stop and have a more lengthy discussion if participants want it.

Method of debriefing

1. Immediately following an exercise, before stopping for a break, gather all participants in a quiet and confidential area.

© Teresa Williams 1991, from 'Effective Debriefing – The key to learning', published by the British Association for Commercial and Industrial Education, 1991.

2. Explain that you want participants to chart up, without talking to anyone else, how they are feeling at the moment.
3. Issue them with a strip of paper as shown below.

Drawing 1a

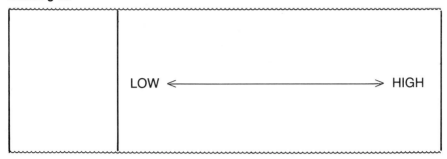

4. Ask participants to write in their name and put a cross representing their level of morale.

   An example of how the strips should be completed is given in drawing 1b. This is for your use only. Do not show participants the example.

Drawing 1b

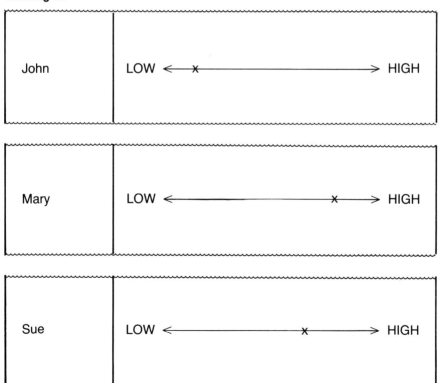

© Teresa Williams 1991, from 'Effective Debriefing – The key to learning', published by the British Association for Commercial and Industrial Education, 1991.

5. Ask participants to pin up their strips. Make sure they have written their names on them.
6. Look at where participants have put their crosses before conducting a discussion. Select your approach in the light of any unexpected results. Look for those participants with very high or very low scores and consider how you are going to explore what led to these results. Remember to ask those with middle scores how their morale could have been increased.
7. Remember to go only as deep in the debriefing as participants can accept.
8. Decide whether you need to go on with the debriefing using another method or whether all relevant items have been covered.

Variations

1. Participants can plot their feelings at particular points during an exercise.
2. This style of debriefing can be used at the end of a training day. You can ask participants to complete a strip for the beginning, the middle and the end of the day.

© Teresa Williams 1991, from 'Effective Debriefing – The key to learning', published by the British Association for Commercial and Industrial Education, 1991.

Style 2: Sketching feedback

General description

This method of debriefing enables particular aspects of a group's performance to be shared. Sketching the feedback symbolically instead of using words helps not only to give variety to the feedback process but helps to make it easier for participants to express their ideas.

Applications

This method can be used immediately after an exercise, at the end of a training day, or at any point where participants need to look at how they are working as a group. It can be used to assist participants to distinguish between factors that helped the task and factors which helped the group to work together. Sketching helps to stimulate the debriefing process particularly if previous methods have been written or verbal.

Time

Participants will need about 15 to 20 minutes to complete their sketches and then at least 5 minutes each to show and explain their sketches. Further time may be needed at the end to draw any common threads together or to work on any common difficulties.

Number of participants

Up to 10 participants.

Other considerations

This can lead to quite a lengthy debriefing session and is not something that can be rushed. If participants are thinking on quite a deep level they may require more reflection time before they are able to express themselves symbolically. Those who say they have no artistic ability should be encouraged to use simple diagrammatic pictures. Remind them that it is the ideas which are important and not the standard of drawing.

© Teresa Williams 1991, from 'Effective Debriefing – The key to learning', published by the British Association for Commercial and Industrial Education, 1991.

Method of debriefing

1. Explain that you want participants to think about the exercise in which they have just participated in terms of 3 specific areas:

    - the success or failure of the task itself
    - how the group worked together
    - their own contribution

    Show them drawing 2.

Drawing 2

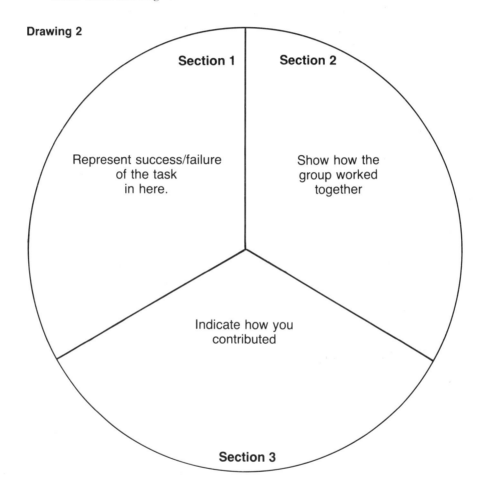

2. Explain that you want participants to complete their circle by sketching their replies in the relevant section rather than by writing them. Remind them that their standard of drawing does not matter.
3. Issue them with flipchart paper and pens and let them go and find a quiet place somewhere on their own. Set an agreed time limit for return eg 20 minutes.

© Teresa Williams 1991, from 'Effective Debriefing – The key to learning', published by the British Association for Commercial and Industrial Education, 1991.

4. Check that all participants have finished and then pin up the completed sheets.
5. There are two main ways for participants to explain their charts:
   - To focus on each separate issue and compare ideas easily, take everyone's section one first, section two second, and section three last.
   - To link how individuals view the situation as a whole, take each participant's chart as a whole.
6. Remember to go only as deeply in the debriefing as participants can accept.
7. Decide whether you now need to go on with the debriefing using another method or whether all relevant items have been covered.

Variations

1. You can substitute any other topics eg a high point, a low point, something that helped or something that hindered.
2. If participants have been working in sub-groups they can present joint sketches to the other sub-groups.

© Teresa Williams 1991, from 'Effective Debriefing – The key to learning', published by the British Association for Commercial and Industrial Education, 1991.

Style 3: Meeting review

General description

This method of debriefing is suitable for involving participants in deciding how to debrief a meeting which has been filmed on closed circuit television. It is particularly appropriate for a mature group who are used to taking more responsibility for their learning process and who have some experience of attending and running meetings.

Application

This method can be used where participants have some experience of running and attending meetings and can relate the theory to practical application. For example experienced managers would find it useful during a refresher session on their meetings skills.

Time

Participants will need about 45 minutes to decide on what basis they will observe and review an exercise. They will then need up to one hour to apply that review process.

Number of participants

Up to 8 participants.

Other considerations

You may need to allow more time for the debriefing process if participants are able and willing to benefit from a more in-depth feedback session. Participants may need occasional guidance to keep to relevant and important items. They may also need help to keep the session balanced ie not to spend a disproportional amount of time on any one item.

© Teresa Williams 1991, from 'Effective Debriefing – The key to learning', published by the British Association for Commercial and Industrial Education, 1991.

Method of debriefing

1. Explain to participants that they will be taking part in a meeting which will be filmed using closed circuit television.
2. Explain that before they start the meeting you would like them to decide what aspects of running and contributing to meetings they want to review afterwards.
3. Help participants to draw up an appropriate observer's checklist which they will use while watching the playback of their meeting.
4. Help participants to decide how they want the feedback and review session to be run. What points in particular do they want covered, in what order and by what method? You should give guidance to participants to ensure that their suggestions will result in a constructive session.
5. Film the meeting.
6. Play back the film of the meeting encouraging participants to observe themselves using their own observer's checklist.
7. Help participants to conduct the review session using their previously agreed method. You should ensure that the session remains constructive.
8. Remember to let participants go only as deeply as they can accept.

Variations

1. You can substitute any other topics that have been filmed eg interviews or role plays.
2. After the debriefing participants can film another attempt at a similar subject and measure their improvement.

© Teresa Williams 1991, from 'Effective Debriefing – The key to learning', published by the British Association for Commercial and Industrial Education, 1991.

Style 4: Involved/frustrated

General description

This method of debriefing focuses participants' minds on a set of common words to express their feelings. Individuals select the words which best describe their feelings and they then share their list of words with the others.

Applications

This method of debriefing can release tensions and frustrations before they become bottled up. It can also capture feelings before they become rationalised or suppressed. It should be used only once or, at the most, twice in a course. It can be used between an exercise and the main debriefing.

Time

About 10 minutes.

Number of participants

Up to 12 participants.

Other considerations

You need to decide how controlled you intend to keep this session. You need to decide whether you are simply letting the participants air their feelings or whether you are going to expand into why they have those feelings.

This method is useful if you have participants who tend to rationalise their feelings and responses fairly rapidly. With these individuals you need to capture their emotions immediately or else later discussion can be rather shallow.

Method of debriefing

1. Immediately after a challenging exercise gather all the participants together. Ask them not to start discussing the exercise yet.
2. Explain that you want to get their immediate reactions to help with more in depth feedback after a coffee break.

© Teresa Williams 1991, from 'Effective Debriefing – The key to learning', published by the British Association for Commercial and Industrial Education, 1991.

3. Ask participants to decide which words best describe how they are feeling. They should write these on cards which can be displayed and easily moved around eg magnetic cards, cards with Velcro, or cards pinned with drawing pins.
4. When everyone has finished ask participants to stick their cards up on the display board.
5. You can group similar word sections together or ask participants to do so.
6. You now need to look at the overall picture being presented by these participants. Decide how to deal with any individual reactions which are widely contrasting to those of the rest of the group.
7. Choose whether to give participants a break at this point or whether to help them to understand what happened during the activity by having an immediate full debriefing session.

   If participants were particularly annoyed, frustrated, or felt left out during the exercise you may wish to help them explore what led to that and to establish how they or the group could have helped. If participants feel particularly exhilarated, successful, or challenged they may need an immediate break to let them calm down. It is only after they have calmed down that they will be able to analyse what led up to those feelings and establish how they can encourage a successful outcome in future activities.
8. Remember to go only as deeply in the debriefing as participants can accept.

Variations

1. If you get participants to initial all their cards you can first group the cards according to the words and then group according to the person or sub-groups.
2. You can ask participants to explain why they selected those particular words as they pin the cards up.
3. You can ask the other participants to give their reactions as each card is put up.

© Teresa Williams 1991, from 'Effective Debriefing – The key to learning', published by the British Association for Commercial and Industrial Education, 1991.

Style 5: Debriefing planning

General description

This method of debriefing helps participants explore the way in which they planned how to tackle an exercise. It will help them to focus on specific issues, to discuss and debrief, rather than just having a rambling discussion.

Applications

This method can be used by participants at any level of experience of planning. It can be used to help them look at aspects of planning with which they have difficulty or aspects of planning which you or their managers have observed that they tend to overlook.

Time

Allow at least 30 minutes for debriefing those who are new to planning and considerably longer for those with more experience and who are likely to welcome a more detailed discussion.

Number of participants

Up to 12 participants.

Other considerations

This method can be usefully combined with input from a tutor on specific techniques and ideas relevant to the planning process. You need to find out how many planning techniques and methods participants are already aware of in order to decide how much tutor input is appropriate.

Method of debriefing

1. You may wish to let the participants consider how well the group planned how to tackle the exercise. You can give them time for this by combining it with a coffee/rest break.
2. Then show them your pre-prepared flipchart which indicates the areas you would like them to consider. Ask them if there are any other areas they want to add to the list.

© Teresa Williams 1991, from 'Effective Debriefing – The key to learning', published by the British Association for Commercial and Industrial Education, 1991.

Pre-prepared flipchart for planning

	Non-existent	Done Poorly ⟵⟶	Done thoroughly
Set clear objectives			
Made a clear plan at the start			
Set timetables			
Set deadlines			
Contingency plans made			
Planned method of monitoring and review			

3. When you have the complete list ask all the participants to mark on the chart how well they considered the group did on each point.
4. Encourage the group to explore reasons why some items were done well and others forgotten.
5. Ask the group to conclude their analysis by writing up a checklist of how they would tackle the planning phase of a similar exercise in the future.
6. Try to stay in the background and let the group do their own exploration and analysis. Supply observations and comments only when they are wasting time on irrelevant points or when they do not know what to do next. Also help out if a major learning point is not going to get discussed. Provide specific help if participants ask for it but try to encourage them to take a responsible role in analysing what happened.
7. Remember to go only as deeply in the debriefing as participants can accept.

Variations

1. With a group which has some experience of being debriefed you can explain at the start what you want them to analyse and leave them to follow it through. Check that they keep to the point and remain practical and constructive.
2. This approach can be used with any other topic. Simply substitute the relevant list of points to analyse eg organisation of the team, management of time, how problems were identified and solved.

© Teresa Williams 1991, from 'Effective Debriefing – The key to learning', published by the British Association for Commercial and Industrial Education, 1991.

Style 6: Good and bad points

General description

This method of debriefing focuses participants' attention onto which parts of the exercise they found particularly good or particularly bad. It does so in a more interesting way so as to add contrast and variety to your training methods and help keep participants stimulated and interested.

Applications

This method can be used by participants of all levels of experience. It is particularly appropriate when they have had an exercise with a lot of mental work and would appreciate a more relaxed and informal debrief.

Time

Allow at least 20 minutes for participants to prepare their feedback and then allow at least 10 minutes for each participant to show and explain their views.

Number of participants

Up to 8 participants.

Other considerations

Some participants may have difficulty in thinking of a good point if they have had a frustrating experience. Similarly, some participants may have difficulty in thinking of the worst point if they have been exhilarated and elated with success. You should be prepared to help individuals who do have difficulty in focusing on a good or bad point.

Method of debriefing

1. After the exercise check whether participants feel the need to spend some time on their own to reflect on what they have just done.
2. Explain that you would like them to reflect on the exercise which they have just completed and consider the best point and the worst point of the exercise for them (rather than for the group as a whole).
3. Show them the pre-prepared flipchart which you would like them to complete.

© Teresa Williams 1991, from 'Effective Debriefing – The key to learning', published by the British Association for Commercial and Industrial Education, 1991.

Pre-prepared flip chart for 'good points and bad'.

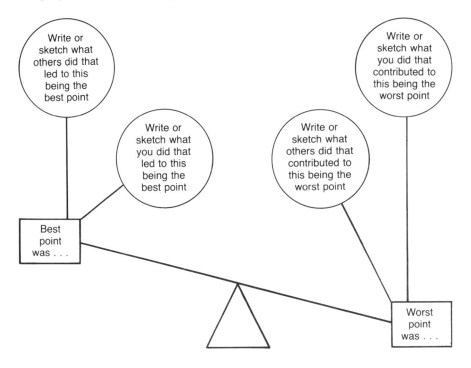

4. Agree a time when they should return with their completed flipchart. (This would depend on how much reflection time they need but would usually be about 20 to 30 minutes.)
5. Issue flipchart paper and pens.
6. Let participants disperse to a quiet place nearby.
7. Walk around and see the sort of points which participants are writing up. If the comments are mostly straightforward then prepare for a fairly brief discussion. If there are unexpected, unusual, or controversial items being raised then plan for a more detailed/counselling type feedback session.
8. Let participants pin up and explain their charts.

Variations

1. This approach can be used with any other topic. Simply substitute the relevant list of points to analyse eg best and worst point about problem solving in terms of what you did and others did, high and low point of communication in terms of what you did that contributed to making it so and what others did.
2. You can ask each participant to complete a similar chart for the best and worst points for the group as a whole. They can then compare and contrast the charts and look for the reasons behind various perceptions.

© Teresa Williams 1991, from 'Effective Debriefing – The key to learning', published by the British Association for Commercial and Industrial Education, 1991.

Style 7: Task and process

General description

This method of debriefing focuses participants' attention on what happened during an exercise in terms of the task itself and the way in which the group worked together.

Applications

This method offers a gentle introduction to the difference between 'task' and 'process' by a common experience. It is useful with groups who find conceptual or theoretical sessions difficult to accept.

Time

Allow at least 20 minutes for participants to prepare their feedback and then allow at least 20 minutes for consolidating the ideas.

Number of participants

Up to 12 participants.

Other considerations

If you have a group of task rather than people orientated participants then this session can lose its impact because the tutor may have to fill in the gaps in the information provided. This can result in participants being less willing to accept the ideas being put forward.

Method of debriefing

1. After the exercise explain that you would like participants to consider the successful aspects of the exercise which they have just taken part in.
2. Explain that you would like them to write on cards words which describe successful aspects of what took place. The cards should be easily moveable once displayed eg magnetic cards, cards with Velcro or cards pinned up with drawing pins.
3. Make sure that there is only one idea per card.

© Teresa Williams 1991, from 'Effective Debriefing – The key to learning', published by the British Association for Commercial and Industrial Education, 1991.

4. Agree a time for completion eg 15 minutes, and encourage participants to work on their own.
5. Issue cards and pens.
6. Let participants disperse to a quiet place nearby.
7. Walk around and see the sort of points which participants are writing up. If the points are mostly to do with the task itself then encourage them to consider other aspects. Do not use the terms 'task' or 'process' at this point.
8. Let participants display their cards on the board.
9. You should now sort the cards into 2 piles. In one pile put those which directly helped getting the task done eg clear objectives, timescales set, or materials checked. In the other pile put those which were concerned about the way in which the group worked together well eg listened to ideas, gave praise or co-operated well.

    (If there are any remaining cards which you feel do not fit into either of these two categories put them in a pile on their own and discuss them at the end.)
10. Now explain why you have sorted them into these two groups and relate to general management theories on how successful groups operate.

Variations

1. You can use a similar approach to explore factors contributing to motivation or management style.

© Teresa Williams 1991, from 'Effective Debriefing – The key to learning', published by the British Association for Commercial and Industrial Education, 1991.

Style 8: Situation analysis

General description

This method of debriefing should be used to help participants to analyse a part of an exercise from several different perspectives.

Applications

This method should be used to help participants gain an insight into how other people see the same situation. It is useful with individuals who have a very 'black and white' approach. It can also help those who were very engrossed with their own role and did not gain a wider view of the situation.

Time

Allow at least 1 hour for a detailed analysis and discussion. Allow at least 15 minutes for reflection and relaxation afterwards.

Number of participants

Up to 10 participants.

Other considerations

This method is more effective when the group has built up a reasonable level of trust and mutual respect. Participants should also be in a frame of mind where they are prepared to listen to each other even if what is being said is totally different to their own ideas.

Method of debriefing

1. During an exercise you or an observer should identify various points at which the participants are obviously not working in a co-ordinated way with the same viewpoint or approach. This may be apparent where different members of the same group inadvertently hinder progress by not being aware of how others are feeling, or reacting to what is taking place.
2. Afterwards, ask participants on which particular part of the exercise they would find it helpful to have views from other people, on what happened

© Teresa Williams 1991, from 'Effective Debriefing – The key to learning', published by the British Association for Commercial and Industrial Education, 1991.

and why. You can help them to make this decision by suggesting some of the scenes which have been identified.
3. When you have agreed one or two significant scenes, start by asking the leader of the group what happened from his or her point of view. Ask the leader to describe what he or she intended to happen and what actually happened.
4. Then ask each participant how they felt at that point and what they thought was supposed to be happening. Get them to focus on the effect it had from their point of view.
5. If there was an observer let him/her describe the observed behaviour, and its effects on the task and the group.
6. Ensure that participants keep the debriefing constructive and helpful. Assist them to respect one another's viewpoints.
7. Guide participants into recording learning points for themselves as individuals which they can apply in similar situations in the future.
8. Allow at least 15 minutes for reflection and relaxation.

Variations
1. This approach can be backed up with the use of closed circuit television.
2. If you feel that participants would benefit by analysing a particular part of an exercise then draw their attention to that part.

© Teresa Williams 1991, from 'Effective Debriefing – The key to learning', published by the British Association for Commercial and Industrial Education, 1991.

Style 9: Question and answers

General description

This method of debriefing helps participants to analyse and check their answers to a question which the tutor has asked them to discuss. This is as suitable for a technical training session as it is for a management training session.

Applications

This method shows a variety of ways in which information from participants can be handled and debriefed. Often tutors will split participants into two or more groups and ask them to discuss a particular question eg what are the advantages of long term planning, or, how can employees be motivated within existing constraints in their organisation? Participants come back with a list of points they have drawn up and look to the tutor to 'pull the threads together'.

The methods given below can be applied when there are correct or desired answers to the question put to participants. They can also be used when there are no totally right answers but you just want to help them to think constructively about the possibilities.

Time

Allow between 20 minutes to one hour depending on participants' interest and the depth to which you want to encourage discussion.

Number of participants

Up to 15 participants.

Other considerations

This method is very suitable for use in the early stages of a course where participants do not know each other well. It can help them learn about each other and encourage an exchange of views on factual topics, so building trust and respect for times when more sensitive issues are being dealt with.

© Teresa Williams 1991, from 'Effective Debriefing – The key to learning', published by the British Association for Commercial and Industrial Education, 1991.

Method of debriefing

1. Recall participants after they have discussed the particular question.
2. Depending on the learning objectives of the participants choose one of the following ways of debriefing:
   (a) If there is a correct or desired approach then ask each group to list the key points of their discussion and to explain them to the other groups. You should then identify and reinforce the key points which you feel are important, giving reasons and explanations. Point out anything which is missing. This method also helps you to build on what participants know already and to spend time only on the things which have been forgotten or were not known.
   (b) If participants find a checklist useful, ask each group to list the key points of their discussion and to explain them to the other groups. Then ask all participants to help categorise the points so that the best or most important points can be turned into a checklist. Participants should be encouraged to use this checklist back at work.
   (c) If you have participants who are interested only in models and theories based on their ideas, ask each group to list the key points of their discussion and to explain them to the other groups. You can then use their information and ideas to lead into relevant theories or models which you want to explain.
   (d) If you want to use ideas from participants as a starting point for helping them to identify problems, advantages, difficulties or benefits, ask each group to list the key points of their discussion and to explain them to the other groups.

© Teresa Williams 1991, from 'Effective Debriefing – The key to learning', published by the British Association for Commercial and Industrial Education, 1991.

Style 10: With a leader and an observer

General description

This method of debriefing is suitable for use with an activity where a leader and observer(s) have been appointed. It provides a systematic method for dealing with feedback.

Applications

This method can be used by participants at any level of experience of a particular subject. It is useful where you want to help participants learn from each other with minimal guiding and steering from you. It is particularly useful where the leader at an early stage in the debriefing process has a need to express his or her satisfaction or dissatisfaction with his or her own contribution to the activity.

Time

Allow at least 45 minutes for a session of reasonable depth with participants who are fairly inexperienced in the subject matter and considerably longer, eg up to 2 hours, for a more open, trusting, and involved debriefing session.

Number of participants

Up to 9 participants.

Other considerations

This method needs observers who are good at listening and noting salient points. This leaves the tutor free to guide and steer the session and participants to learn from each other.

© Teresa Williams 1991, from 'Effective Debriefing – The key to learning', published by the British Association for Commercial and Industrial Education, 1991.

Method of debriefing

1. After the activity sit participants round in a circle or semi circle so that they can see each other.
2. Explain how you would like the debriefing to be conducted. Explain that you will ask the leader for his or her opinions first, and then the observers will lead the feedback session.
3. Give some guidance as to how long you think the debriefing is likely to take.
4. Ask the leader to give his or her opinion as to how well the activity went from his or her point of view. Find out if there is any aspect on which he or she would particularly welcome feedback or discussion.
5. Encourage the observer(s) to follow up what the leader says by going through their observations in a logical order. You may need to help them to decide what constitutes an appropriate order.
6. Encourage other participants to join in the session giving their observations and ideas.
7. Steer and guide this whole process by making sure that participants do not receive more information than they can usefully handle. Encourage participants both to discuss points constructively and to recognise when to stop giving feedback.
8. Help the group to summarise what has been learnt.
9. Ask individuals to spend a few minutes on their own deciding what they are going to do about the information they have received.

Variations

1. You can use closed circuit television to play back examples of behaviour which participants were unaware of.
2. You can state at the beginning of the activity which particular aspects will be reviewed or you can ask participants to decide what would be of most help to them.
3. You could ask participants to review in chronological order, or to concentrate on helpful behaviours and areas for improvement.

© Teresa Williams 1991, from 'Effective Debriefing – The key to learning', published by the British Association for Commercial and Industrial Education, 1991.

Part Four

Questions to ask

You can use the questions in this part to help you to run a debriefing session. You should select one or a combination of questions depending on the particular aspects of management which you want participants to focus on. There are topic questions and general questions for you to choose from.

The information on the topic sheets is based on the techniques described in the earlier parts of this manual. The questions have been designed to help you to apply the ideas on debriefing to different aspects of management training. The questions are NOT listed in order of importance.

You can ask any of the questions as general questions to the whole group. You can also opt to divide participants into syndicate groups to discuss the questions and prepare points to explain to the others. Sometimes you may want to direct a question to a particular individual.

Select the appropriate questions and adapt where necessary to meet the needs of the participants. Use these sheets as a source of ideas. Do not feel constrained by the wording given.

© Teresa Williams 1991, from 'Effective Debriefing – The key to learning', published by the British Association for Commercial and Industrial Education, 1991.

Hot seat   +   1 to 1 (Cocktail)
- group offer feedback to   6 mins (3 each)
individual, 1 min. each   Feedback intense but can no control

Topic questions

Examples of questions you can use:
When debriefing the planning of an activity or task

How did you plan?

What factors helped planning?

What factors hindered planning?

How do you feel others contributed to the planning?

How could others have better helped the planning process?

© Teresa Williams 1991, from 'Effective Debriefing – The key to learning', published by the British Association for Commercial and Industrial Education, 1991.

On what criteria are you judging the success of your plan?

How well did you listen to each other's ideas?

What evidence was there of:
- building on each other's ideas?
- destroying/ignoring each other's ideas?

What did the leader do to help the planning process?

How were objectives/the task explained?

What goals were set?

How were the goals communicated?

© Teresa Williams 1991, from 'Effective Debriefing – The key to learning', published by the British Association for Commercial and Industrial Education, 1991.

Examples of questions you can use:
When debriefing problem solving aspects of an activity or task

Was the problem clearly identified?

How did you set about explaining:
- the problem?
- the constraints?
- the opportunities?
- the resources available?

How were alternative solutions explained?

How were solutions evaluated?

What contributed to effective problem solving?

© Teresa Williams 1991, from 'Effective Debriefing – The key to learning', published by the British Association for Commercial and Industrial Education, 1991.

How did participants work together?

What was the effect on the success of the problem solving?

What was the effect of difficulties/setbacks on:
- the technical solution?
- morale and relationships?

What hindered more effective problem solving from taking place?

How could the blocks to problem solving have been removed or overcome?

What effect did the leader's style have on the way in which the group worked?

How did each individual contribute to the problem solving process?

© Teresa Williams 1991, from 'Effective Debriefing – The key to learning', published by the British Association for Commercial and Industrial Education, 1991.

How could each individual have been more effective in their contribution?

© Teresa Williams 1991, from 'Effective Debriefing – The key to learning', published by the British Association for Commercial and Industrial Education, 1991.

Examples of questions you can use:
For the debriefing of teamwork during an activity or task

How did each individual contribute?

What were the needs of team members?

How did the leader and/or other team members help to meet these needs?

How was conflict dealt with?

What factors led to effective team work?

How could the team work be improved?

© Teresa Williams 1991, from 'Effective Debriefing – The key to learning', published by the British Association for Commercial and Industrial Education, 1991.

How did you feel the group worked as a team?

What factors hindered more effective teamwork?

What this team needs to......

[STOP]

[START]

[CONTINUE]

© Teresa Williams 1991, from 'Effective Debriefing – The key to learning', published by the British Association for Commercial and Industrial Education, 1991.

Examples of questions you can use:

When debriefing the leadership of an activity or task

What style of leadership did the leader adopt?

What was the effect of this style on:
- the task?
- the group?
- individuals?

What factors affected the success/failure of the leader's approach?

What would each individual have liked more of or less of from the leader?

How did you feel as leader?

© Teresa Williams 1991, from 'Effective Debriefing – The key to learning', published by the British Association for Commercial and Industrial Education, 1991.

What feedback would you like on your approach and contribution as leader?

How did you feel participants responded to your approach?

What could participants have done to help you as leader?

What did you find rewarding as leader?

What did you find frustrating as leader?

© Teresa Williams 1991, from 'Effective Debriefing – The key to learning', published by the British Association for Commercial and Industrial Education, 1991.

Examples of questions you can use:

When debriefing the monitoring and control of an activity or task

What monitoring took place?
By whom?

What control was needed?

How did you identify what monitoring and control was needed?

Were group members aware of the monitoring and control process?

© Teresa Williams 1991, from 'Effective Debriefing – The key to learning', published by the British Association for Commercial and Industrial Education, 1991.

What effect did the monitoring and control process have on participants?

What are the implications for monitoring and control in your workplace?

How were the effects of monitoring and control seen by participants? Why?

What systems of control can you develop to help monitoring and control?

How acceptable are these systems likely to be in your workplace?

© Teresa Williams 1991, from 'Effective Debriefing – The key to learning', published by the British Association for Commercial and Industrial Education, 1991.

Examples of questions you can use:

When debriefing decision making which took place during an activity or task

How were decisions made?

What was the effect of this style of decision making?

How did each individual contribute to the decision making process?

What factors helped decisions to be made:
- quickly?
- effectively?

What factors hindered:
- the quality of decisions?
- the speed of decision making?

© Teresa Williams 1991, from 'Effective Debriefing – The key to learning', published by the British Association for Commercial and Industrial Education, 1991.

How were decisions explained?

How were decisions implemented?

How did the style of decision making complement:
- the task?
- the individuals?
- the resources available?

Did the decisions lead to the expected results?
Why?

© Teresa Williams 1991, from 'Effective Debriefing – The key to learning', published by the British Association for Commercial and Industrial Education, 1991.

General Questions

Examples of general questions you can use during debriefing

Particular point

What did you do at the point when . . . ?
What did you notice others doing when . . . ?
At what point did you feel that you were . . . ?

Now

How does that make you feel now?
What are you doing to cope with that?
What would you like from the group to help you?

Future action or change

How can you develop that idea back at work?
What implications are there if you do it that way?
What can you do to overcome those barriers to putting your ideas into action?

Facts

What information helped?
What information hindered?
How did you collect the facts on which to make that decision?
Give some specific examples of fact collecting.

Feelings and emotions

How does that make you feel?
What were the effects of your emotions on the rest of the group at that point?
What prevented you from saying you felt that way at the time?

© Teresa Williams 1991, from 'Effective Debriefing – The key to learning', published by the British Association for Commercial and Industrial Education, 1991.

Quantitative

How often did that happen?
How many times did you notice (participant's name) doing . . . ?

Evaluation

How are you judging success/failure?
What things are you going to evaluate?
What will be valuable to you to evaluate?

Group

How did the group work together?
What did individuals do that helped the group to operate successfully?
What hindered the group from being more effective?

Individual

What effect did that have on individuals?
What effect did that have on you?
What effect did you have on (participant's name) at that point?

Leader

What did the leader do that contributed to success?
What style did the leader adopt?
What effect did the leader's style have on you?
In which ways was the leader's style appropriate?

Positive

What were the positive effects of the group doing . . . ?
What positive behaviour from the leader helped constructive ideas to keep flowing?
How did individuals cope positively with adversity?

Negative

What led to a negative spirit being fostered?
How were negative attitudes expressed?

© Teresa Williams 1991, from 'Effective Debriefing – The key to learning', published by the British Association for Commercial and Industrial Education, 1991.

Descriptive

You looked alarmed when (participant's name) suggested . . . how were you really feeling? Why?

The group seemed to split into two after . . . how did individuals feel about that?

© Teresa Williams 1991, from 'Effective Debriefing – The key to learning', published by the British Association for Commercial and Industrial Education, 1991.